God's Special Rule

Written by Marjorie Redford and Courtney Rice
Illustrated by Scott Burroughs

Based on Matthew 7:12

ISBN 978-1-4143-9300-1

Printed in the United States of America

20
7   6   5

Tyndale House Publishers, Inc.
Carol Stream, Illinois

I am learning a special rule.

Do you want to learn it too?

It's all about loving others,

just as God wants us to do.

You look very hungry.

What if I were hungry too?

I'd want someone to bring me food,

so I'll give food to you.

You look busy at your work.

What if I had a big job too?

I'd want someone to clean with me,

so I will clean with you.

You look as if you've lost a toy.

What if I'd lost my toy too?

I'd want someone to share with me,
so I will share with you.

You look as if you just fell down.

What if I tripped and fell too?

I'd want someone to help me up,
so I'll lend a hand to you.

You look as if you're feeling sad.

What if I were that sad too?

I'd want a friend to talk with me,

so I will talk with you.

You look as if you're getting sick.

What if I got sick now too?